D1088677

# Alligators

by Nancy Furstinger

Content Consultant
James W. Hicks, PhD
Professor of Biology
University of California, Irvine

Core Library

An Imprint of Abdo Publishing
www.abdopublishing.com

www.abdopublishing.com

Published by Abdo Publishing, a division of ABDO, PO Box 398166, Minneapolis, Minnesota 55439. Copyright © 2015 by Abdo Consulting Group, Inc. International copyrights reserved in all countries. No part of this book may be reproduced in any form without written permission from the publisher. Core Library™ is a trademark and logo of Abdo Publishing.

Printed in the United States of America, North Mankato, Minnesota
032014
092014

THIS BOOK CONTAINS
RECYCLED MATERIALS

Cover Photo: iStockphoto/Thinkstock
Interior Photos: iStockphoto/Thinkstock, 1; Juan Gracia/Shutterstock Images, 4; Animals Animals/SuperStock, 7 (top); iStockphoto/Thinkstock, 7 (top middle); Gary Ombler/DK Images, 7 (bottom middle); Eric Isselee/Shutterstock Images, 7 (bottom); Jo Crebbin/ Shutterstock Images, 9, 43; David Huntley Creative/Shutterstock Images, 10; Stock Connection/SuperStock, 13; Monchai Tudsamalee/Shutterstock Images, 15; Larry Lynch/ iStockphoto, 16; Jared Hobbs/All Canada Photos/SuperStock, 18; Fernando Cortes/ Shutterstock Images, 20; Mark Higgins/Shutterstock Images, 22; Shutterstock Images, 24, 36, 40, 45; Melvyn Longhurst/SuperStock, 26; Red Line Editorial, 29; Raffaella Calzoni/ Shutterstock Images, 30; J L Rodriguez/iStockphoto, 32; iStockphoto, 34; NaturePL/ SuperStock, 38

Editor: Mirella Miller
Series Designer: Becky Daum

Library of Congress Control Number: 2014902277

Cataloging-in-Publication Data
Furstinger, Nancy.
 Alligators / Nancy Furstinger.
   p. cm. -- (Amazing reptiles)
Includes bibliographical references and index.
ISBN 978-1-62403-368-1
1. Alligators--Juvenile literature.   I. Title.
597.98/4--dc23
                                          2014902277

# CONTENTS

# CHAPTER ONE

# The Amazing Alligator

As the sun sinks low in Everglades National Park, wild hogs slurp water from the marsh. One hog searches the sand for turtle eggs. A log drifts closer. Suddenly the log shoots straight out of the water. Watch out! It's an alligator!

The big reptile clamps its jaws around the startled hog. Then the gator starts a death roll. It spins with the hog underwater. As it rolls, the alligator rips off

Alligators spend many hours lurking in the water, waiting for prey to appear.

## Muddy Dragons

During the mid-1500s, Spanish explorers in North America spotted a giant alligator. They called this reptile *el lagarto*. This means "the lizard" in Spanish. English-speaking explorers changed the word to *alligator*. The Chinese thought alligators looked like dragons. They called them *tu long*, which means "muddy dragon."

chunks of the hog and gulps them down. The other hogs scatter. The alligator finishes his snack and settles back into the water. He'll hide and wait for his next prey.

There are only two alligator species on Earth—American alligators and Chinese alligators. American alligators are much larger than their Chinese cousins. They are the largest reptiles in North America. Males grow up to 15 feet (4.5 m) long. The biggest can weigh up to 1,000 pounds (454 kg). Females can grow up to ten feet (3 m) long. Chinese alligators are much smaller. Males grow to approximately five feet (1.5 m) long. Females are around 4.5 feet (1.5 m). This species weighs around 90 pounds (41 kg).

Chinese alligator
hatchling
8 inches (20 cm) long

American alligator
hatchling
12 inches (30 cm) long

Adult Chinese
alligator
5 feet (1.5 m) long

Adult American
alligator
15 feet (4.5 m) long

## Sizing Up Gators

The American alligator is much larger than the Chinese species. This size difference can be seen in hatchlings too. American hatchlings are bigger than Chinese hatchlings. How might the size of these two species affect how they hunt and what they eat?

# Living Dinosaurs

Alligators are dark green or black with white bellies.

Their bodies are covered with rows of thick scales.

These scales are called scutes. They protect alligators

from injury and prevent their skin from drying out.

Alligators are an ancient species. Their relatives

evolved approximately 180 million years ago.

These early alligators were on Earth before the dinosaurs! Alligators survived after the dinosaurs died out approximately 65 million years ago.

## Alligator vs. Crocodile

Alligators and crocodiles belong to the same group of reptiles, called *Crocodylia*. How can you tell them apart? Alligators have rounded snouts shaped like a U. Crocodiles have V-shaped snouts. When an alligator's mouth is closed, only its top teeth are visible. This is because its lower jaw is smaller than its upper jaw. When a crocodile's mouth is closed, both its top and bottom teeth show. Crocodiles also have a tooth that juts up from their lower jaw.

## Fierce Predators

Alligators have powerful jaws to crush bones. They have a biting force equal to the weight of a small truck. Each jaw is lined with 80 pointed teeth. Each time an alligator loses a tooth, a new one grows in. They can regrow new teeth up to 50 times. That is thousands of teeth in a lifetime.

Alligators may be big, but they have tiny brains. An alligator's brain is approximately the size

Alligators seem to have an endless supply of teeth.

of half a tablespoon. Alligators rely on their speed and strength to snag their meals. Patience is another advantage. Alligators wait for hours for their prey to appear.

Gators are fierce predators. They are ready to hunt for food from the moment they hatch. But young alligators struggle to survive. They are prey for bigger predators. The biggest threat for young alligators is adult alligators. They are cannibals!

# CHAPTER TWO

# The Biggest Survivors

**M**any alligators from both the American and Chinese species do not reach adulthood. Those that escape predators and grow to four feet (1.2 m) long have a chance to reach old age. These gators can live approximately 50 years in the wild. They can live up to 70 years in captivity.

Although there are many alligator eggs in each nest, a large percentage of hatchlings do not reach adulthood.

## Mating Season

Chinese alligators mate when they are four or five years old. American alligators are ready to mate when they grow to be six feet (2 m) long, usually between 10 and 12 years old.

Neither species have vocal cords. The male, or bull, still puts on a noisy show when he's ready to mate, however. He hopes to attract females, or cows. The bull sucks air into his lungs. Then he blows it out in a roar. He also slaps his head against the water. All of this noise scares away other males.

## Baby Gators

After American alligators mate in the spring, the female builds her nest. She makes a tall mound of mud, sticks, plants, and soil. Then she lays approximately 40 eggs.

## Ancient Alligator

Muja is the world's oldest alligator. He has lived in Serbia's Belgrade Zoo since 1937. This American alligator is a real survivor. He managed to stay alive during the bombing of Belgrade in World War II (1939–1945). Muja is now more than 75 years old!

Male alligators rise out of the water and make lots of noise to attract female alligators.

She covers her eggs with soil and plants to keep them warm. Chinese alligators mate in the summer. They lay between 10 and 50 eggs.

The eggs from both species are ready to hatch in two months. Each baby alligator has what is called an egg tooth. The baby uses this tooth on the tip

**13**

of its snout to slit open the egg. Baby gators are called hatchlings once they leave their shells. An estimated 24 American alligator hatchlings survive from each nest. They make chirping sounds to call their mother. She digs open the nest to free her hatchlings. If a hatchling can't break open its own shell, the mother gently bites open the shell.

The mother leads the hatchlings to water. She also lets them ride in her mouth! The hatchlings have bright yellow stripes. This helps them blend in with grasses and sunlight. They also have needle-sharp teeth. Baby alligators can bite from the second they hatch. They hunt for bugs, tadpoles, and small fish.

Hatchlings are able to get out of their shells on their own using their egg teeth.

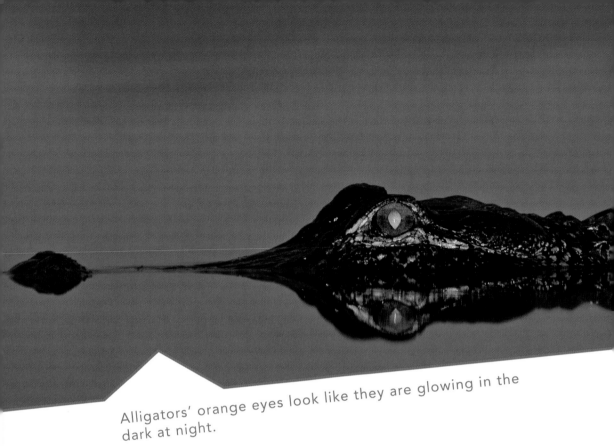

Alligators' orange eyes look like they are glowing in the dark at night.

A pod, or group, of hatchlings stays with its mother for up to two years. Mother alligators protect their babies. But the babies still face danger. Only about ten hatchlings live to be one year old. Wading birds, fish, turtles, snakes, and raccoons gobble up the gators. Bigger and older gators also turn hatchlings into meals. In fact, bigger alligators eat about 7 percent of hatchlings! Scientists are not sure why adult alligators eat hatchlings. But researchers think it might help manage the size of the population.

## Daily Lives

Alligators are nocturnal. This means they are most active at night. That is when they hunt. Their eyes reflect any light that shines on them. This gives alligators great night vision.

## FURTHER EVIDENCE

There is quite a bit of information about mother alligators in Chapter Two. What was one of the chapter's main points? What evidence was given to support that point? Check out the website at the link below. Choose a quote from the website that relates to this chapter. Does this quote support the author's main point? Does it make a new point? Write a few sentences explaining how the quote you found relates to this chapter.

### Alligator Mothers
www.mycorelibrary.com/alligators

# CHAPTER THREE

# Adaptable Reptiles

**A**lligators can live on land and in water. They have three different ways of moving on land. They can high walk by rising tall on their toes and moving slowly. They can belly walk by slithering when they want to slide into water. And they can belly run to escape danger. This kind of running is a faster version of the belly walk. Alligators can move up to ten miles per hour (17 km/h) on land.

Alligators spend their time out of the water basking in the sun and sleeping.

Alligators are able to swim with their eyes open because a clear eyelid protects each eye.

Alligators are great swimmers. They can swim twice as fast as they run. They propel themselves through water by moving their long, powerful tails from side to side. Webbed feet also help them swim. Although gators cannot breathe underwater, they can stay under for up to two hours. Their heart rate slows down and their bodies use less oxygen.

Alligators become watertight when they are underwater. Flaps of skin close off their ears, nostrils, and the backs of their throats. This lets them catch fish without gulping down water. A clear third eyelid protects an alligator's eyes like goggles.

## Patient Predators

Alligators lurk in the water, patiently waiting for their next meal. They are most active from dusk to dawn. During this time they float for hours. Only their eyes, ears, and nose stick above the water's surface.

Alligators use their keen night vision and senses of hearing and smell to seek out prey. They always ambush their victims from the water.

An alligator will lunge quickly if something splashes near its head. Prey in low-hanging tree branches are also in danger. Alligators can use

### Skin Sensors

Alligators have thousands of tiny bumps on their jaws. These bumps detect tiny vibrations in the water. This lets alligators zero in on swimming fish or animals pausing for a drink. The bumps send signals to the alligator to attack when the water is disturbed. The bumps are so sensitive they can sense one droplet of water!

Gators wait patiently to attack at the right moment.

their tails to spring up to five feet (1.5 m) out of the water.

Both American and Chinese alligators have a varied diet. The American alligator chomps down on fish, frogs, turtles, birds, and mammals. Chinese alligators eat clams, snails, fish, birds, and small mammals.

An alligator's blunt teeth are perfect for getting a strong grip on its meal. The teeth are dull, not sharp. But they are ideal for crushing turtle shells and can break bones. Alligators can gobble small prey in one gulp. They drown larger prey using a death roll.

## Surviving an Attack

Alligators rarely attack people. The odds of an alligator attacking a person in Florida, where most encounters occur, are 1 in 24 million. Alligators have killed only one dozen people in the Southeast since 1948. To escape from an alligator on land, experts advise moving away in a straight line as fast as possible. Punch the snout or poke the eyes if you are in water. Alligators prefer easy prey. They are likely to release victims that put up a fight.

Alligators can go an entire year without eating. Instead they get energy from the sun.

As an alligator spins, it tears off chunks of its prey. Alligators cannot chew. They swallow rocks to help grind up their food.

Unlike people, alligators do not eat three meals each day. They might eat once or twice per week. They store any extra calories as fat at the base of their tails. Alligators do not need the energy from food to keep warm. They use the sun to warm their bodies.

Before 1854, a European scientist contacted *Harper's Magazine* requesting a live alligator to examine. In this 1854 article, a writer describes how they responded:

> We made a public appeal through the press in behalf of 'a specimen;' and were not only accommodated by kind neighbors with several of the desirable age and condition, but some one . . . had a monster of many extra feet in length, in the dead hour of the night, fastened at our door, whose huge jaws . . . opened wide enough to swallow any philosopher who would dare to interfere with his habits or dental fixtures. Two alligators, however, we shipped to Gottingen or its neighborhood. They were simply secured in boxes affording plenty of air. . . . By the aid of steamboats, ships, and railcars, they finally, after various adventures through the long period of nearly five months, in good health reached the destined owner.
>
> Source: "The Alligator." Harper's Magazine. Dec. 1854: 37–68. Print. 43.

## Consider Your Audience

Read this passage closely. How would you adapt it for a different audience, such as your classmates, your parents, or younger friends? Write a blog post explaining the information in this passage to the new audience.

# CHAPTER FOUR

# Alligator Habitats

**A**lligators live in freshwater areas. Unlike many crocodiles, alligators cannot survive in saltwater. They thrive in slow-moving rivers and streams. They also live in ponds, swamps, marshes, ditches, canals, and lakes.

Alligators are camouflaged in their watery homes. Their skin is the same color as the water. This helps

Both species of alligators live in freshwater areas around the world.

them blend in. Their prey probably mistakes them for floating logs.

American alligators live where the water and air temperatures are warm. They have a huge habitat across the southeastern United States. Their range begins in North Carolina. Then it runs down along the Atlantic Coast to the tip of Florida. It extends west along the Gulf of Mexico to Texas. Florida and Louisiana have more alligators than any other states. The alligator is the official state reptile of Florida, Louisiana, and Mississippi.

Chinese alligators live in eastern China. Their range once covered a large area of the country. Today they are confined

## The Only Spot on Earth

The marshy wetlands at the southern tip of Florida are a national treasure. This area is called Everglades National Park. It is home to many species. This is the only place in nature where both alligators and crocodiles live together. It is also the only spot in the United States where the American crocodile lives.

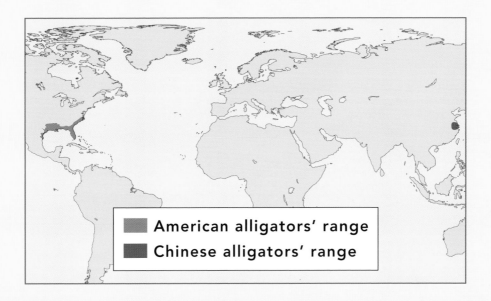

**Alligator Ranges**

Alligators live in two distinct regions. They prefer warm, freshwater spots. This map shows where the American and Chinese alligators make their homes. Why might alligators live in these regions? Write several sentences describing an alligator's habitat.

to a tiny area in the lower basin of the Yangtze River. This river runs along the Pacific coastline.

## Warm Climate

Like all reptiles, alligators are cold-blooded. This means their body temperature varies according to their surroundings. They prefer a warm environment. They bask in the sun to stay warm. When they get too hot, they cool off in the water. They also open their

Going into the water will help lower alligators' body temperatures, but they can also open their mouths to cool down.

mouths wide to let heat escape, just like a dog does when it is panting.

Alligators are able to tolerate colder temperatures than crocodiles. In fact, alligators are pushing their boundaries northward. In the United States, they are expanding into Virginia.

Alligators that live in places with cold winters have found ways to survive. They dig burrows using their snouts and clawed feet. They hibernate, or sleep on and off, for several months. They are sluggish and wake up every so often to eat. Alligators become active again when breeding season starts.

## EXPLORE ONLINE

The focus in Chapter Four is alligator habitats. The website below also discusses alligator home ranges. As you know, every source is different. How is the information given in the website different from the information given in this chapter? How is it the same? What new information can you learn from this website?

### Alligator Habitats
www.mycorelibrary.com/alligators

# CHAPTER FIVE

# Predator Becomes Prey

Adult alligators are fierce predators. They have very few natural enemies. Occasionally jaguars or leopards will kill an alligator.

In the Everglades, pythons are another predator. The Everglades are marshy wetlands in southern Florida that are home to many alligators. Many people abandon pet pythons in the Everglades when they become too big. These giant snakes from Southeast

Alligators are at the top of the food chain but can be threatened by pythons in the Everglades.

Many albino alligators live in captivity. This helps them survive longer since they struggle to survive in the wild.

Asia can grow to be 17 feet (5 m) or longer! Tens of thousands of these snakes live in the Everglades. Sometimes pythons swallow alligators whole. But alligators sometimes win the battle and eat the snake.

One rare type of alligator has more predators than others of its kind. Approximately 50 albino alligators live in the United States. These white reptiles are unable to blend into their backgrounds. They lack camouflage. These gators do not survive very long in the wild.

Many creatures other than adult alligators prey on baby alligators. Herons and raccoons also make meals of hatchlings.

## Saved from the Brink

Humans are alligators' most dangerous threat. People hunt alligators. There is a huge demand for their skins. People use alligator hide to make bags, belts, and boots. Alligator eggs and teeth also bring high prices. People eat gator meat too.

By 1967 American alligators were listed as an endangered species. They were in danger of becoming extinct. Conservation groups and wildlife agencies worked to protect these reptiles. They conducted research. They funded studies to examine every stage of the alligators' life cycle. They also studied their habitats.

American alligators made an amazing recovery while the government protected them. They grew in numbers. In 1987 the US Fish and Wildlife Service

Alligators are now commonly seen in the southeastern United States after making a comeback from the endangered species list.

removed alligators from the endangered list. Today about 5 million alligators live in the Southeast.

People continue to harvest alligators. The demand for their hides and meat is met in several ways. Some states have an alligator-hunting season. Each state carefully controls the number of alligators taken. The 30-day hunting season is important for some people in Louisiana. Some people also raise alligators on farms. People in southeastern states collect eggs in the wild and sell them to farms. The farms raise the gators. Once the eggs hatch and the alligators get bigger, the alligators' hides and meat are sold.

Habitat loss is another danger facing alligators. People drain wetlands where alligators live in order to develop the land for roads and buildings. Another problem is rising sea levels due to climate change. This could cause saltwater to flood alligators' freshwater homes. Alligators usually live in freshwater near the places where rivers drain into oceans.

## Endangered in the Wild

Chinese alligators face a giant struggle. They are critically endangered.

### Alligator Wrestling

The Seminole are a Native American tribe living in Florida. They are famous for wrestling alligators. After wrestling alligators to capture them, these Native Americans brought the gators back to their camps for food. When tourists started coming to Florida in the 1900s, wrestling shows became an attraction. Alligator wrestling is dangerous. Bare-handed wrestlers battle gators for ten minutes. Participants sometimes win more than $10,000 in prize money along with bragging rights.

Very few Chinese alligators live in the wild. Their habitats are being destroyed, leaving them no place safe to live.

Fewer than 130 of these reptiles survive in the wild. People have destroyed their habitat. They have built dams and drained wetlands. Then they pump the water into nearby cities and use it to grow rice. Alligators have been forced to move from rivers to ditches and ponds. They eat fish and ducks raised by farmers. This upsets the farmers, who then kill the alligators.

Although there are few Chinese alligators in the wild, they are making a comeback in captivity. Research centers have been breeding these animals.

The largest center has ponds with 10,000 alligators! Each year more than 1,000 eggs hatch. The first captive-born alligators were released into the wild in 2003. But they have a long way to go before they make a recovery like the American alligator. Chinese wetlands will first have to be restored.

## Saving Alligator Species

Alligators outlasted the dinosaurs. Will they continue to thrive in today's climate? Conservation groups are working to make sure these reptiles will survive in the wild. The American alligator is a success story. But the Chinese alligator still faces an uphill struggle.

### Saving Chinese Alligators

Chinese alligators got a helping hand from a New York zoo. Hatchlings born and raised at the Bronx Zoo were reintroduced into China in 2007. Scientists are tracking the alligators using radio transmitters. They discovered the rare reptiles started multiplying in the Yangtze River. This project offers hope that wild populations will increase.

Alligators are amazing reptiles, and it is important for humans to do everything they can to protect them.

Conservation groups also teach people why it is important to protect alligators. These reptiles prevent populations of prey species from growing too high. A reduction in alligators can have a ripple effect. When there are fewer alligators, populations of fish and snakes grow. This throws off the balance of ecosystems.

Alligators are important predators. They have been around for millions of years. Humans must protect freshwater habitats. Then these remarkable reptiles will survive in the wild for years to come!

Nick Wiley, the executive director of the Florida Fish and Wildlife Conservation Commission, discussed the important role hunting fees have played in boosting the alligator population:

> In 1967, the American alligator was listed as an endangered species because of unregulated market hunting. Today alligators are abundant throughout Florida, providing plentiful hunting opportunities. . . . Public hunting of alligators has been allowed in Florida since 1988, and total harvests now average more than 20,000 per year. License and permit fees paid by alligator hunters provide the funding for the science and management that insures sustainable alligator management programs.

Source: "Witnesses Praise Positive Role of Hunting on Conservation and Management." Committee on Science, Space, and Technology. science.house.gov, June 19, 2012. Web. Accessed December 16, 2013.

## Changing Minds

Take a position on alligator hunting in Florida. Imagine your best friend has the opposite opinion. Write an editorial trying to change your friend's mind. Make sure you explain your opinion and your reasons for it. Include facts and details that support your reasons.

**Common Name:** Alligator

**Scientific Name:** *Crocodylia*

**Average Size:** 4.5 to 15 feet (1.5 to 4.5 m) long, depending on species

**Average Weight:** 90 to 1,000 pounds (41 to 454 kg), depending on species

**Color:** Dark green or black with white belly

**Average Life Span:** Up to 50 years in the wild

**Diet:** Fish, frogs, turtles, clams, snails, birds, and mammals

**Habitat:** Warm bodies of fresh water in the southeastern United States and eastern China

**Predators:** Humans, pythons, and other alligators

## Did You Know?

- Alligators cannot chew their prey.
- The first alligators appeared on Earth before dinosaurs.
- An alligator can survive for an entire year without eating.
- American alligators have recovered from their endangered status.

# STOP AND THINK

## Say What?

Learning about alligators can mean learning a lot of new vocabulary. Find five words in this book that you've never seen or heard before. Use a dictionary to find out what they mean. Using your own ideas, write down the meaning of each word. Then use each word in a sentence.

## Another View

There are many different sources of information about alligators. As you know, every source is different. Ask a librarian or another adult to help you find a reliable source about alligators. Write a short essay comparing and contrasting the new source's point of view with the ideas in this book. How are the sources similar? How are the sources different? Why do you think they are similar or different?

## Why Do I Care?

This book discusses the fact that alligators are at the top of the food chain. Even if you don't live near alligators, why should you care about their food chain? Write down two or three reasons humans should care about alligators.

## Surprise Me

Learning about an alligator's life cycle can be interesting and surprising. Think about what you learned from this book. Can you name two or three facts about alligators you found surprising? Write a short paragraph about each fact. Why did you find them surprising?

# GLOSSARY

**albino**
an animal that is born with a lack of pigment, causing it to appear colorless

**camouflage**
patterns or coloring that help disguise or hide an animal

**cannibals**
animals that eat their own kind

**cold-blooded**
unable to regulate body temperature without an outside source, such as the sun

**endangered**
threatened with extinction

**extinction**
the death of all members of a species

**hatchling**
a recently hatched animal

**nocturnal**
most active at night

**predator**
an animal that lives by killing and eating other animals

**prey**
an animal hunted or killed by another animal for food

**scutes**
horny scales

**species**
a group of similar animals that are closely related enough to mate with one another

# LEARN MORE

## Books

Gibbons, Gail. *Alligators and Crocodiles.* New York: Holiday House, 2010.

Gish, Melissa. *Alligators.* Mankato, MN: Creative Education, 2011.

Pringle, Laurence. *Alligators and Crocodiles.* Honesdale, PA: Boyds Mills Press, 2009.

## Websites

To learn more about Amazing Reptiles, visit **booklinks.abdopublishing.com**. These links are routinely monitored and updated to provide the most current information available. Visit **www.mycorelibrary.com** for free additional tools for teachers and students.

# INDEX

# ABOUT THE AUTHOR

Nancy Furstinger is the author of more than 100 books. She has been a feature writer for a daily newspaper, a managing editor of trade and consumer magazines, and an editor at children's book publishing houses. She once paddled alongside alligators while canoeing in Florida.